Mind-Blowing Bakes

WAYLAND

First published in 2012 by Wayland

Copyright © Wayland 2012

Wayland
Hachette Children's Books
338 Euston Road
London NW1 3BR

Wayland Australia
Level 17/207 Kent Street
Sydney NSW 2000

Editor: Debbie Foy
Designer: Lisa Peacock
Photography: Ian Garlick
Proofreader/indexer: Sarah Doughty
Consultant: Sean Connolly

British Library Cataloguing in Publication Data

Professor Cook's mind-blowing bakes.
1. Baking--Juvenile literature. 2. Food--Composition--
Juvenile literature.
I. Mind-blowing bakes
641.8'15-dc23

ISBN: 978 0 7502 6883 7

Printed in China

Wayland is a division of Hachette Children's Books,
an Hachette UK Company.
www.hachette.co.uk

Contents

PROFESSOR COOK'S... INCREDIBLE EDIBLES!

ARE you hungRy to LEARn moRE about youR Food?

Have you ever wondered why some foods behave the way they do? For example, have you ever wondered how simply delicious meringue is made from little old egg whites? Or how ice cream can be baked (yes, baked!) in a hot oven without it melting — not even a little bit? Find out the answers to these questions and more with Professor Cook and the team!

Discover how to make hot ice cream sparkle, cupcakes with an explosive twist and delicious bread baked in a seedy flowerpot! Approach the black & blue buns with caution (only because they are so dangerously nutritious!). Oh, and don't have nightmares over our super-cheesy oozing crust pizza!

HAPPY ~~EXPERIMENTING~~ COOKING!

PROFESSOR COOK'S KITCHEN RULE BOOK

→ Wash your hands before you start cooking and after handling raw stuff, like meat

→ Mop up spills as soon as they happen

→ Use oven gloves for handling hot dishes straight from the oven

→ Listen up! Take care with sharp knives. Don't walk around with them!

→ Switch off the oven or cooker top when you have finished cooking

→ Use separate chopping boards for vegetables and meat

→ Raw and cooked foods should be kept separately in the fridge

→ Don't forget to tidy up the kitchen afterwards! No brainer, huh?

ABBREVIATIONS

g = grammes

tsp = teaspoon

tbsp = tablespoon

ml = millilitres

°C = degrees Celsius

HOT GOODS!

WHEN YOU SEE THIS WARNING SIGN AN ADULT'S HELP MAY BE NEEDED!

The 'Science Bits'

Believe it or not, cooking involves a lot of science! The Science Bits that accompany each of Professor Cook's delicious recipes answer all the mysteries about food that you have ever wanted to know. They also explore some of the interesting, unusual or quirky ways that our food often behaves!

Stuff you need:

100g unsalted butter
125g light soft brown sugar
1 medium egg
1½ tsp vanilla extract
½ tsp baking powder
175g plain flour
50ml buttermilk
1 tbsp red cochineal food colouring
75g cream cheese
225g icing sugar, plus extra
for dusting

Makes 13 pies

HOT GOODS!

These bright red little treats are made with a natural red food colouring and buttermilk — a secret ingredient that makes your cakes deliciously soft — just like velvet!

Step 1

Preheat the oven to 180°C/fan 160°C/gas mark 4. Line two baking sheets with baking paper. Draw round a 5cm plain cookie cutter to mark out 26 light pencil circles on the baking paper. Turn the paper over.

CRIMSuN VELVET WHOuPIE PIES!

Step 2

Beat together 75g butter and all the sugar until pale and fluffy. Add the egg and 1 tsp vanilla extract. Beat again until smooth. Add the baking powder, flour, buttermilk and colouring. Whisk for 1 minute only, until well combined.

Step 3

Drop teaspoonfuls of the cake mixture onto the drawn-out circles and spread until it just fills them. Bake for 12-15 minutes. After 10 minutes cooling, transfer to a wire rack to cool completely.

Step 4

Beat the remaining butter with the cream cheese, remaining vanilla extract and icing sugar. Sandwich the red cakes together with the creamy filling. Dust with icing sugar. Delicious!

The Science Bit

Is cochineal really made from beetles?

Well, yes and no. The stuff we call cochineal is a chemical extract of carminic acid made from the bodies of crushed female scale insects from South and Central America! But they are not beetles. Don't let this put you off cochineal though. This red pigment has been used for centuries by the Aztecs and native Americans!

7

CHOCCY CHOUX PUFFS

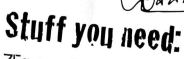

Stuff you need:

75g unsalted butter
60g strong plain flour
2 large eggs, beaten
300ml double cream
1 tbsp icing sugar
75g dark chocolate
75g white chocolate

Makes 8

HOT GOODS!

Choux is pronounced like 'shoe' but is as light and fluffy as a cloud! So how are these so scrumptiously yummy AND so perfectly puffy?

Step 1

Preheat the oven to 200°C/fan 180°C/gas mark 6. Place 50g of butter into a pan and add 150ml water. Heat until the butter melts, then turn up the heat until the water boils. Remove the pan from the heat and add all the flour. Beat with a wooden spoon until the mixture forms a soft ball in the centre of the pan. Allow to cool.

Step 2

Whisk the beaten eggs, a spoonful at a time, into the cooled mixture until smooth. Place evenly spaced spoonfuls of mixture onto two wet baking sheets. Bake for 10 minutes, then increase the oven temperature to 220°C/fan 200°C/gas mark 7. Bake for a further 15 minutes. Remove from the oven and transfer to a wire rack. Make a slit in the sides of the buns to allow the steam to escape.

Step 3

Whip the cream until thick and stir in the icing sugar. Spoon into the split buns.

The Science Bit

What makes choux pastry so puffy?

Choux has a high water content and when it is baked in the oven, the water evaporates to form steam. But that steam cannot escape because the protein in the eggs binds the outside of the dough 'balloon' so that it remains puffy once you have let the air escape from the slit!

Step 4

Roughly chop the white and dark chocolate. Melt each in separate bowls over a pan of hot water, with half of the remaining butter added to each bowl. Allow to cool for 10 minutes before dipping the buns in the melted chocolate. Sprinkle with flaked chocolate to decorate!

EXPLODING CUPCAKES!

Popping candy is a cracking good topping to sprinkle on your cupcakes! But where does popping candy get its big bang?

HOT GOODS!

Step 1

Preheat the oven to 180°C/fan 160°C /gas mark 4. Line two bun tins with paper cases. Place all the cupcake ingredients into a bowl and whisk for 2 minutes.

Step 2

Divide the mixture evenly between the cases. Bake for 18-20 minutes until golden. Transfer to a wire rack to cool.

Step 3

For the frosting, beat the butter and icing sugar until smooth. Add the vanilla and 2-3 tbsp hot water and beat again. Divide the mixture into bowls and add a few drops of food colouring to each bowl.

Step 4

Use a piping bag to add swirls of frosting on to your cupcakes. Sprinkle with popping candy and edible glitter. Eat straight away for cakes that are sure to be a blast!

The Science Bit

What gives popping candy its big bang?

Popping candy is made like other hard candy, except that carbon dioxide (CO_2) is added at high pressure when the mixture of sugar, lactose, corn syrup and flavourings have been heated to boiling point. The CO_2 stays 'trapped' in bubbles, with walls that harden as the candy cools. When the candy hits your tongue and melts, the high-pressure CO_2 escapes with a loud 'pop'!

Stuff you need:

450g puff pastry, thawed if frozen
2 tbsp plain flour, for dusting
400g tin custard
1 tsp vanilla extract
Grated rind of 1 lemon
2 medium eggs
25g icing sugar

Makes 10 tarts

HOT GOODS!

An egg is a giant single cell, just like the cells that make up your body!

The Science Bit

How does custard change from a liquid to a solid?

The process of changing a liquid protein (the custard) to a solid (the set custard filling) is called coagulation, and this is done by heating. Custard is a mixture of eggs, milk and sugar. When heated, the protein in the eggs and milk coagulate to change the texture of the food.

SQUIDGY WIDGY CUSTARD TARTS

Crisp on the outside and squidgy on the inside – these custard tarts are irresistible. One will not be enough!

Step 1

Preheat the oven to 190°C/ fan 170°C/gas mark 5. Roll out the pastry on a floured surface to 1cm thick and 30 x 40cm in area. Cut out 10 circles of about 10cm diameter. Use them to line a muffin tin.

Step 2

Whisk together the custard, vanilla, lemon rind and eggs and pour into the pastry cases. Bake for 35-40 minutes until the filling is set. Allow to cool completely before transferring them to a baking tray.

Step 3

Dust the tarts thickly with icing sugar and grill under a high heat for 2 minutes or until the sugar starts to brown and caramelize.

OOZING CRUST PIZZA

This pizza features stretchy mozzarella cheese as a topping but also as a filling for the pizza crust. Cheese-o-rama!

Stuff you need:

145g pizza base mix
1 tbsp flour, for dusting
1 ball mozzarella cheese, diced
2 tbsp sun dried tomato paste
4 cherry plum tomatoes, halved
Handful fresh basil leaves

Serves 2

HOT GOODS!

Step 1

Preheat the oven to 220°C/ fan 200°C/gas mark 7. Make the pizza base mix according to the instructions. Knead the dough on a lightly floured surface until smooth and elastic. Press out into a 25cm circle.

Step 2

Arrange half the mozzarella around the dough edge in a circle about 1cm in. Wet the edge of the dough and gently lift it over the cheese. Press down to enclose it all the way around. Allow the dough to prove in a warm place for 15 minutes.

Step 3

Spread the tomato paste over the pizza base and add the remaining mozzarella, cherry tomatoes and basil leaves over the top. Bake for 12-15 minutes until the cheese has melted.

As you heat MOZZARELLA the proteins uncoil and become stringy and elastic!

The Science Bit

Cheese gives you nightmares: science fact or urban myth?

If you go to bed with a full stomach, you may spend more of the night in REM (rapid eye movement) sleep, which is when your most vivid dreams occur. But there is no evidence to suggest that cheese causes your dreams to be bad.
Conclusion: URBAN MYTH!

VERY BERRY CHOCO RIPPLE MERINGUES

These snowy peaks of magic are made from a combination of everyday ingredients. Crisp on the outside and chewy on the inside, the texture is simply irresistible!

Stuff you need:

3 egg whites
175g caster sugar
2 tbsp cocoa powder
300ml whipped cream
Mixed fresh berries

Makes 6

Step 1

Preheat the oven to 120°C/fan 100°C/gas mark 1/2. Whisk the egg whites with an electric hand whisk until just stiff. You should be able to hold the bowl over your head without any falling out! While whisking, add the sugar a spoonful at a time until the meringue becomes thick and glossy.

Step 2

Sift the cocoa powder over the meringue and fold in with a metal spoon to achieve a 'rippled' effect.

Step 3

Line a baking sheet with baking paper and spoon on 6 piles of meringue. Bake for 2 hours. Turn the oven off and leave the meringues in the oven for a further hour. Serve piled with whipped cream and fresh berries!

THE CRISPNESS OF MERINGUE DEPENDS ON HOW MUCH SUGAR IS BEATEN INTO THE EGG WHITES!

The Science Bit

Can meringues ever change back into egg whites?

No. When we whisk egg whites we are breaking down the protein chains in the structure of the egg white. This process is called 'denaturing'. As the denaturing of protein cannot be reversed, this process is known as an irreversible change. So, meringues, listen up! You will never be egg whites again!

KITCHEN SINK POT PIES

Everything-but-the-kitchen-sink can be thrown in to these yummy pot pies to really get your tastebuds a-jangling!

Step 1

Whizz the flour and butter in a food processor until the mixture resembles fine breadcrumbs. Add **4-5 tbsp** water until the mixture forms a pastry. Allow to chill for 30 minutes.

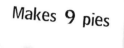

Step 2

Preheat the oven to **200°C/ fan 180°C/ gas mark 6**. Roll out two-thirds of the pastry and use a **10cm** cutter to stamp out **9** circles to line a muffin tin.

Step 3

Fry the bacon, chicken and thyme over a medium heat for 7-8 minutes, stirring occasionally until cooked through. Stir in the cheese and apple sauce. Spoon the mixture into pastry cases.

The Science Bit

What is 'umami'?

Umami is one of the 5 flavours (including salt, sweet, sour and bitter) that human beings can detect through receptor cells on their tongues. The word 'umami' was first used by a Japanese professor who discovered that various foods contained this savoury, meaty flavour. Foods with a high umami content are red meats, fish such as anchovies, sardines and tuna, seafood, soy sauce, tomatoes and cheese.

Step 4

Roll out the remaining pastry and stamp out 9 x 8-cm circles. Wet the edges of the circles and press them down firmly onto the filled pastry cases. Brush the pie tops with beaten egg and season with salt and pepper. Bake for 25-30 minutes until golden. Allow to cool in the tin for 10-15 minutes before tucking in!

HOT ICE CREAM SPARKLE

Stuff you need:

2 chocolate muffins
500ml ice cream
4 medium eggs
225g caster sugar
Edible glitter sprinkles

Serves 4

HOT GOODS!

How can you bake ice cream in a hot oven without it melting? Make this amazing hot-but-cold dessert, then serve it to your friends!

The Science Bit

How can you bake ice cream without it melting?

When we whisk up meringue we make loads of little pockets of air in the mixture! When the meringue is spooned over the ice cream all those nifty air pockets acts as insulators which prevent warm air from getting inside and melting the ice cream! The heat from the oven also starts to caramelize the sugar in the meringue and forms a delicious golden brown crust on the outside, which forms a protective layer over the ice cream, too. Bingo!

Step 1

Halve the muffins horizontally and place the 4 pieces equally spaced onto a baking sheet. Pile a quarter of the ice cream over each muffin and place in the freezer until ready to use. Preheat the oven to 230°C/fan 210°C/gas mark 8.

Step 2

Whisk the egg whites with an electric hand whisk until they are stiff and will stay in the bowl when it is upturned! While whisking, add the sugar a spoonful at a time. The meringue will become white, thick and glossy.

Step 3

Cover the muffins and ice cream with the meringue, working quickly before the ice cream melts. Ensure you 'fill in' any holes that will allow heat in to melt the ice cream. Bake immediately for 3-4 minutes until golden brown. Sprinkle with edible glitter and serve.

SUPER SEEDY FLOWERPOT BREAD

You don't even need to be a green-fingered gardener to watch these delicious mini flowerpot loaves grow. All you need to do is awaken the yeast!

Step 1

Preheat the oven to 220°C/fan 200°C/gas mark 7. Wash the pots in hot soapy water. Rinse and pat dry. Brush them inside and out with oil and place on a baking tray. Bake for 10 minutes. Very carefully remove from the oven and allow to cool completely. Turn off the oven.

Step 2

Brush the insides of the pots with softened butter. Mix all the seeds together and sprinkle half onto the buttery insides. Tip upside down and save any seeds that do not stick.

Stuff you need:

- 6 small, new terracotta flowerpots
- 4 tbsp vegetable oil
- 15g softened butter
- 15g sesame seeds
- 15g poppy seeds
- 25g pumpkin seeds
- 25g sunflower seeds
- 1 tbsp black treacle
- 1 sachet (7g) fast-action dried yeast
- 500g wholemeal bread flour
- 2 tbsp milk

Makes 6 bread pots

HOT GOODS!

Step 3

Mix the treacle with 100ml warm water. Stir in the yeast and allow to sit for 5 minutes to 'foam'. Sift the flour into a bowl and stir in the yeast mixture. Add 400ml warm water and half the remaining seeds. Use your hands to form a soft dough.

Step 4

Knead the dough for 3-4 minutes until smooth. Divide into 6 balls and place into the pots. Brush with milk and scatter over any remaining seeds. Leave the pots to prove in a warm place for 30 minutes until the dough doubles in size. Preheat the oven to 230°C/fan 210°C/ gas mark 8. Bake the pots on a baking tray for 15 -20 minutes. Serve warm or cold.

The Science Bit

Is yeast really a living organism?

Yes it is! Yeast is actually lots of tiny microscopic fungi (mushroom relatives) that are activated by warmth, moisture and sugar. When we leave dough to prove or rise in a warm place, the yeast in the dough converts natural sugars from the flour into gases which are trapped in the bread. These gases are responsible for all the little holes you can see in a slice of bread, and which create pockets for your jam or peanut butter!

STACK 'EM HIGH CHEESY PUFF PIE

What turns a thick cheese sauce into a deliciously light and airy souffle when baked? Read on...

Stuff you need:

75g unsalted butter
25g fine fresh white breadcrumbs
40g plain flour
1/2 tsp English mustard powder
300ml whole milk
100g mature Cheddar cheese, grated
4 large eggs, separated

Serves 6

HOT GOODS!

Step 1

Preheat a baking tray in 200°C/fan 180°C/gas mark 6. Melt 25g of the butter and use it to brush the insides of six 250ml ramekins. Sprinkle with the fine breadcrumbs to coat and set aside.

Step 2

Melt the remaining butter in a saucepan. Add the flour and mustard powder and stir for 1 minute over a low heat. Gradually add the milk and stir until the sauce thickens. Remove from the heat and stir in the cheese and egg yolks. Beat well.

Step 3

Use an electric hand whisk to beat the egg whites until stiff. Stir a large spoonful of whites into the cheese sauce to 'loosen' the mixture. Using a metal spoon gently fold the remaining whites into the sauce. Spoon into the ramekins, filling just to the rim. Clean the ramekin rims with kitchen paper to allow the souffle to rise evenly.

Step 4

Carefully remove the hot baking sheet from the oven and place the ramekins onto it. Bake the mini souffles for 8-10 minutes, until golden. Serve and eat immediately.

The Science Bit

What makes souffle so light and airy?

Air is the most important ingredient in a souffle and is the reason why it rises! When the egg whites are folded into the cheese sauce the fats in the sauce coat the air bubbles in the whites. When heat is applied the air inside the egg whites expands and 'inflates' it. But eat it quickly, because as soon as the air inside is lost the souffle will deflate!

Stuff you need:

15g butter, melted
3 medium eggs
75g caster sugar
125g plain flour
1 tsp easy-blend yeast
50ml warm milk
125g blueberries
150g blackberries
2 tbsp icing sugar

Makes 12

HOT GOODS!

BLUEBERRIES ARE FULL OF ANTi-OxidANTS WhiCh hELP to COMBAT ANd ELiMiNATE TOXiNS iN OUR bodiES

The Science Bit

Why are blueberries so super?

These little purple berries really are a powerhouse of good stuff! One of the top 10 superfoods ever, they are high in vitamin C, anti-oxidants and fibre, all of which are excellent for keeping your skin in good condition as well as fighting diseases like cancer, heart disease and asthma. Scientists also say that blueberries keep your brain more active. Pass the blueberries, please!

BLACK & BLUE BUNS

Don't be fooled by the name of these buns. They are totally and utterly good for you as they contain an amazingly talented superfood...

Step 1

Preheat the oven to 220°C/fan 200°C/gas mark 7. Brush a 12-hole bun tin with melted butter.

Step 2

Whisk together the eggs, sugar and flour until smooth. Mix the yeast and warm milk together until smooth and whisk into the egg mixture. Pour evenly into the prepared bun tin.

Step 3

Scatter the blueberries and blackberries into the centre of each bun. Bake for 12-15 minutes until golden brown. Dust with the icing sugar to serve.

Stuff you need:

175g unsalted butter
200g golden caster sugar
1 medium egg
1 tsp vanilla extract
400g plain flour, plus extra
for dusting
32 plain boiled sweets

Makes 32 cookies

HOT
GOODS!

Human beings are
'PROGRAMMED' through evolution to
enjoy sweet foods!

Stained glass candy in a cookie, all
rolled into one – it's magic!

Step 1

Preheat the oven to 180°C/fan 160°C/gas
mark 4. Line two baking trays with baking paper.
Cream the butter and sugar until pale. Stir in
the egg and vanilla extract. Fold in the flour,
and add 1–2 tbsp water to form a dough. Wrap
the dough in cling film and chill for 30 minutes.

STAINED GLASS COOKIES

Step 2

Unwrap the dough and cut in half. On a floured surface, roll half of the dough to a 3mm thickness. Using 10cm cookie cutters cut shapes from the dough and place on the baking sheets. Repeat with the remaining dough.

Step 3

Use a 3cm cutter to stamp circles from the centre of your cookies and put a boiled sweet into the hole. Bake for 10 minutes. Tilt the tray to allow the melted sweets to fill the holes. Cool for 5 minutes, then transfer to a wire rack to cool completely.

The Science Bit

Are boiled sweets <u>really</u> boiled?

Yes! A boiled sweet is a concentrated sugar solution. As sugar and water are heated, the water boils away and the sugar concentrates as the temperature of the mixture rises. The highest temperature and most concentrated sugar solution results in boiled sweets, which become hard and brittle (rather than chewy) when cooled.

PROFESSOR COOK'S GLOSSARY

ANTI-OXIDANTS substances in our food that help to rid our bodies of toxins, slow down cell damage and protect us from disease

BEAT a quick and vigorous mix with a spoon or whisk

BLEND to mix two or more ingredients together

BUTTERMILK the slightly sour liquid left over after butter has been churned

CARAMELIZE the process that happens to sugar when it is heated. It converts to caramel

CELL basic unit of all living things

COAGULATION when protein molecules or chains rearrange themselves, break or change

EVOLUTION a process of development through which something changes into a different and more complex form

FIBRE a substance found in some foods that adds bulk to our food and aids digestion

FRY to cook food with oil in a shallow frying pan

FUNGI the name given to a group of living things, which includes yeast for making bread

INSULATOR material or object that does not allow heat to easily pass through it

IRREVERSIBLE (CHANGES) describes something that cannot be changed back

KNEAD to fold, push and pull dough with your hands until it becomes soft and smooth

MOLECULES the smallest units of a chemical substance or compound

PROTEIN the second most common substance in our body (after water), helping us to grow and fight disease

PROVE when a dough is left in a warm place to rise

RAMEKIN a miniature cooking dish often used for souffles

REM stands for Rapid Eye Movement. It is a deep sleep state in which dreams can occur

SCALE INSECT a type of small insect that produces a waxy coating (the 'scale') as protection

SIEVE to strain a liquid or push something through a sieve to get rid of lumps

SOLUTION a liquid containing a dissolved solid or gas

SUPERFOODS nutrient-rich foods that can help to fight off ageing and illness

TOXINS poisonous substances produced by cells

UMAMI a Japanese word meaning 'pleasant savoury taste'. It is one of the five basic tastes

WHISK to mix something quickly to get air into it

YEAST an agent used to raise dough in breadmaking

INDEX

USEFUL WEBSITES

www.spatulatta.com
Get some basic cooking skills under your belt, with step-by-step video recipes and a recipe box that includes options for cooking a meal by choosing a basic ingredient, a type of food, occasion or particular diet.

www.yummyscience.co.uk
Super-fun science projects to try out in the kitchen using everyday foods. Grow your own crystals with salt, test out the toasting properties of bread or make your own honeycomb toffee. Some of these recipes call for an adult's help, so always make sure you let an adult know before you start.

www.exploratorium.edu/cooking
Find out how a pinch of curiosity can improve your cooking! Explore recipes, activities and webcasts that will improve your understanding of the science behind food and cooking.

Discover some more incredible edibles with PROFESSOR COOK and the team!

Smashing Snacks
9780750268516

Pop-tastic popcorn
Smashing caramel shards
Ice cream in a bag
Cheese-and-ham-o-rama!
Homemade beans on toast
Oat-so yummy power cookies
'No-cry' onion bhajis
Double-dipped mallow cookies
Mini superhero pies!
Gold bullion honeycomb bars!
Pink fizz-bomb lemonade
Big dipper breadsticks
Professor Cook's glossary
Index

Mind-Blowing Bakes
9780750268837

Oozing crust pizza
Stack 'em high cheesy puff pie
Exploding cupcakes
Stained glass cookies
Crimson velvet whoopie pies!
Very berry choco meringues
Kitchen sink pot pies
Hot ice cream sparkle
Super seedy flowerpot bread
Choc pops
Black and blue buns
Squidy widgy custard tarts
Professor Cook's glossary
Index

Dynamite Dinners
9780750268523

Sticky chicky burger stacks
Tex Mex taco salad bowl
Incredible edible bowl soup!
Posh fish 'n' chips 'n' dip!
Pimp your burger!
Finger lickin' chicken satay
Japan-easy tuna rolls
Tongue-tingling sweet and sour noodles
Thirsty couscous cakes!
Scrambly egg fried rice
Superfood cannelloni
Chilli with a deep, dark secret
Professor Cook's glossary
Index

Fascinating Fruits
9780750268844

Tropical fruit with goo-ey chocolate dip
Incredible edible tie-dye lollies
Icy watermelon slices
Hot caramelised pineapple lollies
Super blueberry cheesecake
Homemade yoghurt with fruit squish
'Magic' apple and blackberry pudding
Nicey slicey summer fruit jelly
Wobbly strawberry mousse
Ice bowl fruit salad
Instant frozen yoghurt
Sticky licky banoffee cones
Professor Cook's glossary
Index